The Little B
Story Ba

Using story bags to enhance story telling

By Marianne Sargent

Edited by Sally Featherstone

Illustrations by Martha Hardy

Little Books with ***BIG*** ideas®

Little Books™

Published 2008 by A&C Black Publishers Limited
38 Soho Square, London W1D 3HB
www.acblack.com

First published 2008 by Featherstone Education Limited

ISBN 978-1-9060-2924-1

Series Editor: Sally Featherstone

A CIP record for this publication is available from the British Library.

Printed in Great Britain by Latimer Trend & Company Limited

This book is produced using paper that is made from wood grown in managed, sustainable forests. It is natural, renewable and recyclable. The logging and manufacturing processes conform to the environmental regulations of the country of origin.

Contents

Introduction

This book is aimed at practitioners working with young children in Early Years Foundation Stage settings as well as teachers working in Key Stage 1. It is also a useful resource for parents and carers, offering guidance and ideas on sharing stories with their children.

Reading stories is an invaluable experience for young children, helping them to develop a wide range of important skills. As well as developing listening skills, children who have regular access to stories develop an awareness of story structure, character and setting. They also begin to understand the concept of letter sounds and words printed on the page and increase their vocabulary.

The importance of stories as part of young children's learning is reiterated in the 2007 Statutory Framework for the Early Years Foundation Stage (EYFS). The Educational Programme for Communication, Language and Literacy states;

'Children's learning and competence in communicating, speaking and listening, being read to and beginning to read and write must be supported and extended. They must be provided with opportunity and encouragement to use their skills in a range of situations...' (p13)

Offering opportunities for active, involved, cross-curricular learning, story bags help bring stories to life and offer practical ideas that serve the differing interests and learning styles of young children.

For each of the story bags in this book you will find:

- the title and author of the featured story;
- a list of objects and resources linked with the story;
- a list of suggested activities related to the story;
- suggestions for alternative book titles that cover similar themes;
- a list of additional stories and information books;
- suggestions for useful websites;
- the relevant learning intentions covered in undertaking the activities.

What are story bags and what should they contain?

Story bags are a widely used tool in Foundation Stage settings. They contain a focus story-book as well as any props and characters needed to act the story out. In addition, story bags contain a range of objects, resources and suggested activities that can be linked with the story.

In Communication, Language and Literacy, the Curriculum Guidance for the Foundation Stage 2000 states:

> *'Young children's learning is not compartmentalised. They learn when they make connections between experiences and ideas that are related to any aspect of their life in the setting, at home and in the community. Young children also learn best when they are happy and confident. A love of books and stories, rhymes and poems and a growing interest in rhyming, alliteration, sounds and words, depend on mutual pleasure and enthusiasm in planned and incidental work.' (p45)*

Out of doors

For every story in this book, you will find suggestions for using the story bag out of doors. Outdoor provision is central to the EYFS, and stories told and re-enacted out of doors will have a powerful effect on children's learning and enjoyment.

Make your own...

Don't be put off by being on a tight budget. Pillowcases are inexpensive and can easily be turned into draw-string bags. Also, many of the items featured for inclusion in the sacks can be made by hand. For example, if you do not have plastic fruit, make them out of salt dough and let the children paint them. Collect pictures from magazines, cut up old posters and laminate them. Look in charity shops, go to car boot sales and write to parents and carers asking for unused items.

Tip: Dolls' house furniture can be very useful for story props.

How does the use of story bags link in with the Early Years Foundation Stage Framework?

Accompanying each of the story bags in this book you will find a list of suggested activities that can lead on from the featured text. The specific learning intentions to these activities are also listed. However, the use of story bags in general covers many of the early learning goals.

In **Personal, Social and Emotional Development**:

Continue to be interested, excited and motivated to learn.

Maintain attention, concentrate and sit quietly when appropriate.

In **Communication, Language and Literacy**:

Listen with enjoyment and respond to stories, songs and other music, rhymes and poems and make up their own stories, rhymes and poems.Retell narratives in the correct sequence, drawing on the language patterns of stories.

Know that print carries meaning and, in English, is read from left to right and top to bottom;

Show an understanding of the elements of stories, such as main character, sequence of events and openings and how information can be found in non-fiction texts to answer questions about where, who, why and how.

In **Knowledge and Understanding of the World**:

Investigate objects and materials by using all of their senses as appropriate.

In **Creative Development**:

Use their imagination in art and design, music, dance, imaginative and role-play and stories.

Respond in a variety of ways to what they see, hear, smell, touch and feel.

Story bags as part of the outdoor curriculum

Story bags are just as valuable in the outdoor environment as they are indoors. Stories are not something that should be confined to the indoors, indeed some require a large amount of space in order to be acted out. Imaginative use of outdoor space can lead to exciting settings for retelling stories. Gathering together around the sand or water trays or arranging story props among the plants in the gardening area gives children the opportunity to develop a realistic sense of story setting, stimulating their senses and enhancing their imagination.

The importance of outdoor learning is emphasised in the EYFS document;

> *'Being outdoors offers opportunities for doing things in different ways and on different scales than when indoors... Outdoor environments offer children freedom to explore, use their senses, and be physically active and exuberant.' (Principles into Practice card 3.3)*

With each story featured in this book there is an idea for incorporating outdoor settings for the retelling. Consider the suggested resources carefully and think about how they might be used outside, where the role play area can be based outdoors, drawing and painting activities can be set up at an outdoor table or easel and information books and puzzles can be laid out on a picnic blanket.

Jasper's Beanstalk

A gardening story

What you could put in the bag

* audio version of Jasper's Beanstalk (Hodder Children's Books)
* a variety of dried beans - butter, haricot, kidney, broad
* black and white cuddly toy cat
* children's gardening tools (fork, trowel, watering can)
* children's gardening book
* small plant pots (plastic & clay)
* book about slugs and snails
* plastic slugs and snails
* laminated pictures of beanstalks of different heights
* traditional tale - Jack & the Beanstalk
* children's calendar

What you could do to follow up the story:

1. Act out the story using the props - do this in a gardening role play area or using a tray filled with soil outside.
2. Look closely at the dried beans, talk about similarities and differences, sort them by size, colour, shape.
3. Count the beans or arrange them to form patterns.
4. Use the beans to make a collage.
5. Examine the gardening tools and talk about their uses. Talk about what a gardener does. Set up a garden centre in the role-play area.
6. Plant different beans - use a calendar to keep a check on how long they take to grow.
7. Go on a snail/slug hunt. Talk about what snails look and feel like, how they move, where they live. Find out more using information books.
8. Set up a snail/slug habitat using plastic minibeasts.
9. Make slugs and snails using play dough.
10. Arrange laminated beanstalks in order of height.

More stories to share

Jack and the Beanstalk by Richard Walker & Niamh Sharkey

The Gigantic Turnip by Alexei Tolstoy & Niamh Sharkey - a modern take on the traditional tale with great illustrations.

Fran's Flower by Lisa Bruce & Rosalind Beardshaw - along the same lines as Jasper but Fran tries different foods to make her flower grow.

Web sites

www.bbc.co.uk/gardening - practical ideas for hands on projects.

www.teachingideas.co.uk/pe/beans.htm - for a beany action game.

www.bbc.co.uk/cbeebies/stories - animated version of Jack and the Beanstalk and a fun variation called 'Growing Up'.

Links with the Early Learning Goals

KUW: Look closely at similarities, differences, patterns and change;
find out about and identify some features of living things, objects and events they observe.

PSRN: Count up to six objects;
use language such as 'taller' and 'shorter' to describe size;
order items by height.

PD: Handle tools, objects, malleable materials safely & with increasing control.

CD: Explore colour and shape; make collages.

Elmer

Being different

What you could put in the bag

* toy Elmer & toy grey elephants
* plastic wild animals - elephants, tiger, lion, hippo, zebra and a tree
* small patchwork blanket
* coloured & patterned paper samples
* lots of coloured & textured fabrics cut into shapes
* children's books about feelings
* feelings word cards & mirrors
* jungle/wild animal sounds CD
* dough and patterned rolling pins
* audio version of Elmer and Wilbur available on CD from Red Fox

What you could do to follow up the story:

1. Act out the story using the props - do this outside among the plants or equipment in the garden or outside area.
2. Examine the patchwork blanket and wallpaper samples and talk about colour, shape and pattern.
3. Examine the ready cut patchwork shapes and talk about colour, shape, pattern and texture. Arrange the patchwork shapes to make different patchwork patterns.
4. Talk about how Elmer was feeling. Use information books, mirrors and word cards to make expressions linked with different feelings.
5. Listen to jungle or wild animal sounds and encourage the children to recreate the sounds and movements of different animals.
6. Set up a role play gift shop with a variety of patterned gift wraps, bags and labels.

More stories to share

Any of the other Elmer books would be good alternatives.

Frog is Frog, Max Velthuijs - a book with a message - 'We are all special for different reasons'.

It's Okay to Be Different, Todd Parr - reassures children that individuality is what makes us special.

Web sites

www.bbc.co.uk/cbeebies/rolymo/library - for an animated tale select 'Baby Elephant's Birthday'.

www.hamilton-trust.org.uk - select the Early Years tab.

www.naturegrid.org.uk/infant/earlyict - select 'Stories' and 'Elmer' for a fun and simple ICT lesson plan.

Links with the Early Learning Goals

PSD: Have a developing awareness of their own needs, views and feelings and be sensitive to the needs, views and feelings of others.

PSRN: Talk about, recognise and recreate simple patterns.

KUW: Find out about and identify features of the natural world.

PD: Move with confidence, imagination and safety.

CD: Explore colour and shape; choose particular colours to use for a purpose; make collages.

Dogger

A sharing story

What you could put in the bag

* cuddly soft brown toy dog
* yellow teddy bear with blue ribbon
* dolls of the characters - Dave, Bella, Joe, Mum, Dad, little girl at the fair
* some fake ice creams
* a selection of small toys for the sale - car, doll, small blocks, ball etc
* real coins and price labels
* information books about dogs
* information books about families

What you could do to follow up the story:

1. Act out the story using the props as you sit on beanbags outside.
2. Get the children to bring their favourite toys and talk about how you would feel if they got lost or sold to someone else.
3. Taste different flavoured ice creams and talk about likes and dislikes.
4. Examine the different coins, look at colours, size and shapes. Talk about the values and match to some price labels.
5. Set up a role-play toy stall and price the toys.
6. Help the children organise a real school fair.
7. Use information books about dogs to compare similarities and differences between species.
8. Use the information book about families to talk about different family members, siblings and relationships.

More stories to share

Elmer and the Lost Teddy by David McKee - a lovely story about the heartbreak of a baby elephant when he loses his favourite teddy.

I Love You Blue Kangaroo! by Emma Chichester Clark - another good story about the importance of a little girl's favourite toy.

Olivia and the Missing Toy by Ian Falconer - a useful prompt to talking about lost toys with very cute pictures.

Web sites

www.sparklebox.co.uk - select 'numeracy' and scroll down to 'coins and money' for interactive activities and coin images.

www.bbc.co.uk/northernireland/schools/4_11/hurley/radio - go to 'archived resources' and select 'Hurley-Burley 3' for teachers' notes about toys, including poems and songs.

Links with the Early Learning Goals

PSD: Have a developing awareness of their own needs, views and feelings and be sensitive to the needs, views and feelings of others; express likes and dislikes.

PSRN: Recognise numerals 1 to 9; use language such as 'more' or 'less' to compare two numbers; recognise different coins.

KUW: Find out about and identify some features of living things; find out about past and present events in their own lives, and in those of their families and other people they know.

The Black Geese

A Russian tale

What you could put in the bag

* dolls/figures to represent characters - Mother, Father, Elena, little brother, three friends
* two toy black geese
* old woman doll for Baba Yaga
* fish and shell, squirrel and walnut, mouse and pebble
* hut with three big legs - make this from a cardboard box
* examples or photographs of Russian eggs or nesting dolls
* egg shaped stencils for drawing
* laminated map of Europe or globe
* information books about birds

What you could do to follow up the story:

1. Act out the story using the props as you sit on a picnic blanket outside.
2. Discuss the moral of the tale.
3. Examine the Russian eggs. Paint templates or blown out egg shells.
4. Examine the Russian dolls. Make nesting dolls using different sized paper cups.
5. Look for Russia on the map in relation to the UK; talk about the different sorts of transport that could take you there.
6. Share information books about birds.
7. Make geese collages using real black feathers.
8. Make model geese with wings that flap, or make a bird mobile.

More stories to share

Polina's Day, Andrey Ilyin - a day in the life of a Russian child.

Hidden Tales From Eastern Europe, Antonia Barber & Paul Hess - folk tales from Poland, Slovakia, Russia, Croatia, Serbia, Slovenia & Romania.

I Wonder Why Geese Go On Holiday? and other questions about birds - facts about birds for young children.

Little Daughter of the Snow, Arthur Ransome & Tom Bower - a Russian couple make a little girl out of snow.

Web sites

www.geographia.com/russia - information about Russia - for adults.

www.dltk-kids.com/animals/birds.html - big selection of craft ideas for making all kinds of birds.

www.swgfl.org.uk/belinda - click on the duck for an excellent explanation of the lifecycle of a duck.

Links with the Early Learning Goals

PSD: Have a developing respect for the cultures and beliefs of other people; consider the consequences of their words and actions for themselves and others.

KUW: Find out about and identify some features of living things; select tools and techniques they need to shape, assemble and join materials they are using; begin to know about the cultures and beliefs of other people.

CD: Explore colour, texture, shape and form in two and three dimensions; express and communicate their ideas, thoughts and feelings by designing and making.

Handa's Surprise

Learn about Africa

What you could put in the bag

* CD or DVD of Handa's Surprise, from Walker Books
* small dolls for Handa and Akeyo
* a basket with plastic tropical fruits - banana, guava, orange, mango, pineapple, avocado, passion fruit, tangerines
* small world animals - monkey, ostrich, zebra, elephant, giraffe, antelope, parrot, goat
* information book about African animals and about growing up in Kenya
* animal lotto
* animal puppets
* African music on tape or CD

What you could do to follow up the story:

1. Act out the story using the props - do this outside on a grassy patch on a hot, sunny day.
2. Use the basket and plastic fruit to explore capacity.
3. Examine and taste different tropical fruits. Talk about similarities and differences and likes and dislikes.
4. Make a fruit salad.
5. Why does Handa carry the basket on her head? Find out about the lives of children in Kenya by using an information book or video. Look at similarities and differences. Ask children to think about what life would be like in Africa.
6. Share the information book about African wild animals.
7. Talk about what a surprise is and how it feels to be surprised. Ask children if they have been surprised.
8. Set up a role play fruit and vegetable stall or greengrocer.
9. Dance to African music.

More stories to share

Handa's Hen also by Eileen Browne features a range of wild animals.

Oliver's Fruit Salad by Vivian French & Alison Bartlett - use this book as an introduction to making a fruit cocktail.

Web sites

www.oxfam.org.uk/coolplanet/kidsweb/wakeup - photographs and information about a typical day in the life of a selection of children around the world (including a little boy from Ghana)

Links with the Early Learning Goals

PSD: Be confident to try different fruits; express likes and dislikes; understand that people have different needs, views, cultures and beliefs that need to be treated with respect.

PSRN: Use language such as 'full' and 'empty' to describe capacity.

KUW: Find out about and identify some features of living things; begin to know about their own cultures and beliefs and those of other people.

CD: Imitate and create movement in response to music.

Smiley Shark

A seaside story

What you could put in the bag

* audio version of Smiley Shark, from Little Tiger Press
* toy shark - preferably one with teeth
* selection of plastic tropical fish
* toy fishing boat, fisherman and net
* fishing game
* water/seaside sounds on tape/CD
* natural items from the seaside - shells, pebbles, dried seaweed
* information book about sharks and other sea creatures
* tub of fish/sea creatures for sorting

What you could do to follow up the story:

1. Act out the story using the props - you could do this outside using a water tray.
2. Read the story in a large space and encourage the children to move according to the descriptions in the book (twisting, turning, splashing, dipping, diving, darting, dashing).
3. Paint tropical fish and imaginary sea creatures.
4. Find out about sharks and other sea creatures using the information books.
5. Go on a visit to the seaside.
6. Listen to and describe sounds of the real sea, or on a DVD or tape.
7. Examine and describe some seaside objects, sort and classify them.
8. Make collages with shells, pebbles, seaweed.

More stories to share

Commotion in the Ocean by Giles Andreae & David Wojtowycz - a rhyming seaside book with opportunities for music and movement.

Fun and Games: Shake Rattle Roll - Action Rhymes for Toddlers and Young children by Hilda Offen - more opportunities for movement.

Hooray For Fish by Lucy Cousins - a good rhyming action tale (includes DVD).

Web sites

www.kented.org.uk/ngfl/games - scroll down and select 'sound sea' for an interactive letter recognition game.

www.kidzone.ws/sharks/index.htm - lots of information about sharks and online activities for children.

Links with the Early Learning Goals

KUW: Look closely at similarities, differences, patterns and change; find out about and identify some features of living things; observe, find out about and identify features in the place they live and the natural world.

CLL: Explore and experiment with sounds and words.

PD: Move with confidence, imagination and safety.

CD: Explore colour, texture, shape, form and space - make collages and paint.

Cleversticks

Growing up in China

What you could put in the bag

* small world people to represent characters in the story
* tiny props for each character
* real chopsticks & Chinese bowls
* Information books, pictures, video or DVD about growing up in a Chinese culture
* books about Chinese New Year
* toy dragons
* examples or pictures of Hung Bao - little red packets for gifts of money
* laminated examples of Chinese script with English translations
* traditional Chinese music on CD

What you could do to follow up the story:

1. Act out the story using the props - you could do this indoors on a blanket or outside around a picnic table.
2. Organise a Chinese banquet. Help the children to write invitations, make a shopping list, prepare the food and decorate the setting.
3. Practice eating with chopsticks.
4. Circle time - talk about things the children are good at - can anyone do something special that they could teach everyone else?
5. Share information books about China and Chinese life.
6. Make Chinese New Year Dragons. Dance with them to Chinese music.
7. Set up a role play Chinese restaurant.
8. Make and decorate Hung Bao (little red packets) and count out chocolate or plastic coins to put inside.
9. Examine examples of Chinese script, find out what they mean and how they are read. Try writing some Chinese characters

More stories to share

The Dancing Dragon by Marcia Vaughn & Stanley W Foon - a rhyming story about how Chinese New Year is celebrated complete with a pull out dragon.

Web sites

www.topmarks.co.uk - select 'multicultural ed' and 'Chinese New Year' for information and activities.

www.kented.org.uk/ngfl/games/hongBow_v4.html - use this to make Hung Bao (little red packets).

Links with the Early Learning Goals

PSD: Have a developing respect for the cultures and beliefs of other people; have a developing awareness of their own feelings and be sensitive to the feelings of others.

KUW: Begin to know about the cultures and beliefs of other people.

CLL: Extend their vocabulary, exploring the meanings and sounds of new words.

PSRN: Count reliably up to ten everyday objects.

CD: Explore colour, texture, shape, form and space in three dimensions.PD: Move with confidence, imagination and safety.

The Gruffalo

A woodland tale

What you could put in the bag

* audio version of The Gruffalo - available from Macmillan Audio Books
* little brown furry mouse
* soft toy monster like the Gruffalo
* woodland creatures - fox, owl, snake - these could be finger puppets
* information books about woodland creatures
* rhyming lotto game or rhyming card game
* woodland wildlife sound tape or CD
* monster or woodland puzzle

What you could do to follow up the story:

1. Act out the story using the props - try and find a dark, damp area outside.
2. Listen for the rhyming words and ask the children to think of more. Play rhyming lotto.
3. Talk about how the creatures were feeling in the story. Ask the children what makes them feel scared.
4. Use information books to find out more about woodland creatures.
5. Listen to woodland sounds and encourage the children to imagine what it is like to walk in the woods.
6. Go on a woodland walk.
7. Draw, paint or make the Gruffalo.

More stories to share

I Feel Frightened by Brian Moses & Mike Gordon - a picture book that deals with feeling scared.

The Gruffalo Song and Other Songs by Julia Donaldson - good selection of action songs.

The Wild Britain series of books written by Louise & Richard Spilsbury and published by Heinemann provide information about a wide range of British animals with good quality pictures for children.

Web sites

www.gruffalo.com - select 'fun stuff' for games and activities linked with all Donaldson and Scheffler's books.

www.enchantedlearning.com - scroll down to 'nursery rhymes' for a wide selection of rhyming resources and activities.

Links with the Early Learning Goals

PSD: Have a developing awareness of their own needs, views and feelings and be sensitive to the needs, views and feelings of others.

CLL: Show an awareness of rhyme; continue a rhyming string.

KUW: Find out about and identify features in the place they live and the natural world; find out about their environment and talk about the features they like and dislike.

PD: Handle a range of small equipment; handle tools and objects safely and with increasing control.

CD: Make constructions, paintings and drawings; sing a few simple, familiar songs; begin to move rhythmically.

My Friend Bear

Bears are friends for ever!

What you could put in the bag

* soft bears - one big brown one, one medium and one small yellow one
* doll or figure as the little boy Eddy
* children's information books about bears
* information books about feeling lonely
* teddy bear floor puzzle
* rhyming games, eg Slug in a Jug
* tub of Compare Bears
* selection of laminated outlines of bears for tracing
* soft toy bears of different sizes, types and colours

What you could do to follow up the story:

1. Act out the story using the props - use pot plants, a builders' tray or a well planted area outside to recreate the woodland setting for full body play or play in miniature.
2. Listen for the rhyming words and ask the children to think of more; play rhyming games.
3. Use information books about bears to compare similarities and differences between species.
4. Share and discuss the information book about feeling lonely. Talk about friendships within the setting. Extend children's thinking by talking about kindness, sharing and taking turns.
5. Children could draw or paint pictures of their friends.
6. Invite the children to bring in their teddy bear friends for the day.

More stories to share

It's the Bear and Where's My Teddy? two more stories by Jez Alborough - these books from the same series offer similar learning opportunities.

The Very Lonely Firefly by Eric Carle - brilliantly illustrated alternative that deals with feeling lonely.

Web sites

www.kented.org.uk/ngfl/games/index.htm - scroll down to 'Teddy Bear's Picnic' for simple sound and letter matching games.

www.britishcouncil.org/kids-stories-goldilocks.htm - an animated version of the traditional tale with narrative. Children can elect to read along.

Links with the Early Learning Goals

PSD: Have a developing awareness of their own needs, views and feelings and be sensitive to the needs, views and feelings of others; form good relationships with peers; understanding that there needs to be agreed values and codes of behaviour for groups of people to work together harmoniously.

CLL: Use talk to organise, sequence and clarify thinking, ideas and events; show an awareness of rhyme; continue a rhyming string.

KUW: Find out about and identify some features of living things.

Jingle Bells

A winter's tale

What you could put in the bag

* audio version of Jingle Bells story - available from Collins
* two small soft mice and two miniature stockings; toy rat; soft toy ginger cat
* miniature wrapped parcel
* red ribbon with bell attached
* selection of small bells
* children's Christmas songs on tape or CD
* copy of the song 'Jingle Bells'
* The Christmas Story and Nativity set
* a selection of Christmas themed dough cutters and dough

What you could do to follow up the story:

1. Act out the story using the props - do this outside on a cold winter day.
2. Examine the different bells, look at colours, size and shapes. Ring the bells in turn and compare the different sounds.
3. Sing Jingle Bells and other Christmas songs. Ring bells in time and dance.
4. Play listening games with the bells.
5. Play cat and mouse games.
6. Talk about Father Christmas - ask children to think back and talk about last Christmas.
7. Read the Christmas story and talk about Christian beliefs.
8. Make salt dough Christmas decorations using the dough and cutters.

More stories to share

Lucy & Tom's Christmas by Shirley Hughes - a story about celebrating Christmas in the traditional way with beautiful illustrations.

Father Christmas by Raymond Briggs - classic picture book about what life is like for Santa on Christmas Eve - with beautiful pictures.

Mog's Christmas by Judith Kerr - Christmas from a cat's point of view.

Web sites

www.underfives.co.uk/xmas.html - Christmas activities and craft ideas.

www.enchantedlearning.com/crafts/winter - winter craft activities with step by step instructions.

www.apples4theteacher.com/coloring/pages/christmas/index.html - select 'Fun Christmas Colouring Pages' for pictures to colour.

www.mape.org.uk/ChristmasCrackers/index.htm - find some Christmas clipart here.

Links with the Early Learning Goals

KUW: Begin to know about their own cultures and beliefs and those of other people; find out about past and present events in their own lives and in those of their families and other people they know.

CLL: Use talk to reflect on past experience, linking significant events from own experience and from stories; distinguish one sound from another.

PD: Move with control and coordination; show awareness of space..

CD: Recognise and explore how sounds can be changed; sing simple songs from memory; recognise repeated sounds and sound patterns.

Not Now Bernard

Consequences...

What you could put in the bag

* dolls/figures to represent characters (Dad, Mum, Bernard)
* character props - hammer, jug, paint brush, newspaper, dinner plate, television, comic, toy robot, bed
* soft toy monster
* information book about feeling sad
* information book about families
* monster puzzle

What you could do to follow up the story:

1. Act out the story using the props - use a dolls house or shelter outside.
2. Talk about how Bernard feels when his parents ignore him. Use the information book about feelings to help the children empathise.
3. Talk about how Bernard's parents will feel when they realise he is missing. What might they do?
4. Think about how the story would have been different if Bernard's parents had listened to him.
5. Make 'Missing Person' posters featuring Bernard.
6. Paint, draw or make monster pictures or models.
7. Make monster masks and do monster dances.

More stories to share

Clarence Bean, That's Me by Lauren Child - explores similar issues. Clarence cannot find peace in her household.

Come Away From the Water Shirley by John Burnigham - deals with loneliness. A little girl's parents do nothing but moan at her so she delves into her imagination for company.

Web sites

www.welltown.gov.uk/menu.htm - can be used on the interactive whiteboard. Select 'house' and 'living room' for an interactive activity that helps children to explores different kinds of family and the relationships between family members.

www.bbc.co.uk/scotland/education/health/feelings - very good resource for your interactive whiteboard which can be used as a starting point for discussion about feelings.

Links with the Early Learning Goals

PSD: Have a developing awareness of their own needs, views and feelings and be sensitive to the views, needs and feelings of others.

CLL: Use language to imagine and recreate roles; attempt writing for different purposes, using features of different forms - missing posters.

PD: Handle a range of small equipment; handle tools and objects safely and with increasing control.

CD: Make constructions, paintings and drawings.

My Friend Whale

Thinking about the environment

What you could put in the bag

* doll or figure to be the little boy
* large soft or plastic toy blue whale
* small world whales of different species
* information books about whales and the sea
* information book on whale hunting
* ocean sounds on tape or CD
* ocean songs and rhymes on tape or CD
* listening lotto game
* variety of sea creature sponges for printing, paint and trays

What you could do to follow up the story:

1. Act out the story using the props - do this using a water tray indoors or a paddling pool outside.
2. Play games that focus on the senses.
3. Do blindfolded tasting or smelling (talk about the fact that whales cannot taste or smell).
4. Play listening lotto (whales have excellent hearing).
5. Make a range of vocal sounds (whales squeak, click and whistle).
6. Feel different textures (whales have sensitive skin).
7. Talk about how the little boy feels when his whale friend does not come back.
8. Use information books to find out more about whales.
9. Paint or draw pictures of whales, and help the children make conservation posters.
10. Listen to ocean sounds and pretend to be whales swimming through the deep ocean.

More stories to share

Dear Greenpeace also by Simon James - a little girl finds a whale in her pond.

The Snail and the Whale by Julia Donaldson & Axel Scheffler - a snail and a whale make friends and travel the world.

Web sites

www.enchantedlearning.com/subjects/whales - an informative source of facts for teachers, including pictures of different breeds of whale.

http://www.barefoot-books.com/uk/site/pages/776_generic.php - find a wide variety of ideas and resources linked with conservation.

Links with the Early Learning Goals

KUW: Look closely at similarities, differences, patterns and change;
find out about and identify some features of living things, objects and events they observe.

PSRN: Count up to six objects;
use language such as 'taller' and 'shorter' to describe size;
order items by height.

PD: Handle tools, objects, malleable materials safely & with increasing control.

CD: Explore colour and shape; make collages.

The Dance of the Dinosaurs

A very popular subject

What you could put in the bag

* audio version of The Dance of the Dinosaurs
* small world dinosaurs
* dinosaur figures for the characters, Georgie and Dee
* toy ginger cat
* pictures of stormy weather
* hot air balloon - a ball attached by a string to a plastic boat
* information books about dinosaurs
* CD of lively music to dance to
* tub of dinosaurs for sorting
* wooden dinosaur templates
* balloons

What you could do to follow up the story:

1. Act out the story using the props - spread out a circular multicoloured mat outside and pretend it is the planet. Do this on a dark, windy day.
2. Use information books to find out about dinosaurs and what the world looked like in prehistoric times.
3. Make a dinosaur land from recycled materials to use with small world dinosaurs.
4. Look at weather pictures and talk about children's experiences. Black out a room and help the children to create a storm. Use musical instruments (drums, shakers, glockenspiels, rainsticks) to make rain and thunder sounds and torches for lightening.
5. Play music and recreate the dance of the dinosaurs.
6. Fly a variety of balloons outside on a windy day.

More stories to share

Bumpus Jumpus Dinosaurumpus! by Tony Milton & Guy Parker-Rees - uses onomatopoeic words and offers the same opportunity for dance.

Dinosaurs Galore by Giles Andreae & David Wojtowycz - lively and fun with rhyming prose again offering similar opportunities for dance.

Dinosaur Time by Michael Foreman, a heart-warming story of time travel.

Web sites

www.hamilton-trust.org.uk - select the Early Years tab for very detailed 'dinosaurs' topic web, planning and printable resources.

www.bbc.co.uk/sn/prehistoric_life - select 'picture galleries' for good quality pictures of dinosaurs.

Links with the Early Learning Goals

CLL: Show awareness of rhyme and alliteration; recognise rhythm in spoken words.

KUW: Find out about and identify some features of dinosaurs; know how to operate simple equipment; begin to differentiate between past and present; find out about and identify features in the place they live and the natural world.

PD: Move with confidence, imagination and safety.

CD: Make constructions; explore the different sounds of instruments; imitate and create movement in response to music.

Owl Babies

Feeling scared

What you could put in the bag

* CD or DVD of Owl Babies - from Walker Books
* replica nest
* soft toy mother owl and three baby owls or puppets
* information book about owls
* information book about nocturnal animals
* some bird feathers and laminated pictures of bird species to match
* bird puppets
* nocturnal animals puzzle
* book about feeling scared

What you could do to follow up the story:

1. Act out the story using the props - you could do this outside, using a real tree or a fallen branch.
2. Make owl baby puppets using brown craft feathers and very large wiggly eyes.
3. Circle time - talk about how children feel when parents leave them.
4. Compare feathers from different species of birds and match them to bird pictures.
5. Find out more about owls using information books.
6. Ask the questions - Where was mummy owl when she was gone for so long? What was she doing?
7. Use an information book to find out about nocturnal animals. Imagine what it would be like to live nocturnally.
8. Provide a variety of materials for children to examine and use to build nests.

More stories to share

Little Baa by Kim Lewis - a little lamb is so happy playing he gets separated from his mum.

Hug by Jez Alborough - a baby chimp is looking for his mummy so he can get his HUG!

The Owl Who Was Afraid of the Dark by Jill Tomlinson, a lovely story that deals with feeling scared.

Web sites

www.owlpages.com - useful fact source that teachers can use with a wide range of photographs.

www.barnowltrust.org.uk - select 'About the Barn Owl' and 'Info for Kids'.

Links with the Early Learning Goals

PSD: Separate from main carer with support; show care and concern for self; have a developing awareness of own needs and feelings.

KUW: Look closely at similarities and differences; find out about and identify some features of living things.

PD: Handle a range of small equipment; handle tools and objects safely and with increasing control.

CD: Make puppets; use ideas involving fitting, overlapping, in, out and enclosure.

Dear Zoo

An animal story about choices

What you could put in the bag

* audio version of Dear Zoo, Macmillan Audio Books
* laminated letter to the zoo asking for a pet
* soft toy or plastic wild animals - lion, elephant, giraffe, camel, snake, monkey, frog and puppy
* cage made from a cardboard box
* soft or plastic pet animals
* information books on pet care
* items associated with pets - food bowls, water bottles, toys, collars
* information books, DVD of zoos
* animal face masks
* animal stencils or templates

What you could do to follow up the story:

1. Act out the story using the props - do this anywhere indoors or outside, using a blanket, cushions or bean bags.
2. Recreate the story by doing the following:

   Help the children write a letter to a local zoo asking for a pet.

   Put a different toy animal each day in a cage and discuss whether it would make a good pet. Keep the animals for an interactive dis play and label them with children's thoughts and ideas.

   Help the children to use shoe boxes to make cages for the animals.
3. Why is the dog a perfect pet? Ask children to tell each other about their experiences of pets.
4. Find out about the needs of pets using the information books.
5. Introduce a classroom pet and allow the children to help care for it.
6. Set up a role play pet shop or vet, using soft toy pets and boxes with handles for carrying cages.

More stories to share

My Penguin Osbert by Elizabeth Cody Kimmel & H B Lewis - beautifully illustrated tale about a boy who wants a penguin for Christmas.

Lost and Found by Oliver Jeffers - fantastic book with great illustrations. A little boy finds a penguin at his door.

Web sites

www.rspca.org.uk - select 'education' for a range of teaching resources including very detailed lesson plans with photocopiable sheets for Key Stage 1 that can be adapted for Early Years.

Links with the Early Learning Goals

PSD: Show care and concern for living things.

CLL: Attempt writing for different purposes, using features of different forms - a letter.

KUW: Find out about and identify some features of living things.

PD: Use simple tools to effect changes to the materials.

The Big Wide-Mouthed Frog

A story from down-under

What you could put in the bag

* a big green soft or plastic frog, preferably with a big mouth
* soft or plastic animals for the story - kangaroo, koala, possum, emu, crocodile
* book about Australian animals
* map of the world or globe
* information book about Australia
* laminated copy of the number song Five Little Speckled Frogs
* diagram of the life cycle of a frog
* five green frogs counting glove or finger puppets
* video about personal safety - talking to strangers

What you could do to follow up the story:

1. Act out the story using the props - on a hot, sunny day out of doors, in a dry sandy or gravelled area.
2. Examine the cuddly animals and refer back to the descriptions in the book. Use the information book to find other Australian animals and encourage the children to describe them.
3. Find Australia on the map or globe. Use information books to compare Australia with the UK. Think about different ways to travel to Australia.
4. Find out about the life cycle of a frog.
5. Ask the children to think and talk about why the frog nearly got into trouble. Link this to the video about personal safety. Invite a police officer in to talk about this.
6. Use the glove or five finger puppets to sing Five Little Speckled Frogs.

More stories to share

The Bad-tempered Ladybird by Eric Carle - the ladybird learns a lesson about picking fights with others. A slightly different story, but it can be used to explore similar issues.

Web sites

www.sparklebox.co.uk select 'numeracy' and 'numbers' for downloadable frog number cards and a frog and lily pad counting game.

www.bbc.co.uk/schools/barnabybear - select 'stories' and 'Barnaby Down Under' for an animated e-book about Barnaby Bear's travels in Australia.

Links with the Early Learning Goals

PSD: Show care and concern for self.

CLL: Use a widening range of words to express or elaborate ideas.

PSRN: Enjoy joining in with number rhymes and songs.

KUW: Find out about and identify some features of living things; observe, find out about and identify features in the place they live and the natural world.

Titch

Being youngest isn't always fun!

What you could put in the bag

* dolls or figures for Titch, Mary, Pete
* variety of plant seeds and magnifying glasses
* tub of sorting objects for comparing sizes
* laminated height measuring chart
* children's tape measure
* books about growing up
* Titch stories on DVD - try Amazon
* pictures of people of different ages for sorting and ordering
* people or children sequencing jigsaws and card games

What you could do to follow up the story:

1. Act out the story using the props - do this anywhere outside and invite children to take different roles using real life tricycles etc.
2. Ask children to bring in pictures of themselves at different ages and make a display illustrating their growth.
3. Ask children to share their experiences of having older siblings and how it feels to be the smallest. Is biggest always best? Are older children always nicer, smarter, better?
4. Use the measuring chart to find and record each child's current height. Revisit this later in the year and record their growth.
5. Use information books to find out about growing up - invite a parent in with a new baby and let the children ask questions.
6. Use story items and sorting objects to talk about and compare size.
7. Plant different seeds and find out which grows the biggest. Do the big seeds grow the biggest plants?
8. Examine the different seeds and make comparisons.

More stories to share

All Shapes and Sizes and Annie Rose Is My Little Sister by Shirley Hughes - classic picture books exploring the same theme.

You're Too Small by Shen Roddie & Steve Lavis - the mice are too small to help on the farm.

Web sites

www.ltscotland.org.uk/earlyyears/index.asp - select 'resources', 'illustrations' and 'babies' for illustrations of baby development.

www.bbc.co.uk/schools/scienceclips - click to enter the flash site and select 'ages 5-6' and 'ourselves' for a range of interactive activities.

Links with the Early Learning Goals

PSD: Have a developing awareness of their own needs, views and feelings and be sensitive to the needs, views and feelings of others.

PSRN: Use size language such as 'big' or 'little'; compare heights of children.

KUW: Examine objects and living things to find out more about them; look closely at similarities and differences; ask questions about why things happen and how things work.

PD: Handle tools safely and with increasing control.

Whatever Next!

Is it a dream?

What you could put in the bag

* audio version of Whatever Next! - Macmillan Audio Books
* teddy bears to represent Mummy and Baby bear
* small cardboard box, toy colander, Wellington boots, role play food, small picnic blanket
* soft toy owl
* toy space rockets and aliens
* laminated pictures of planets, stars and moon or luminous stars and moon
* laminated copy of The Teddy Bears' Picnic
* The Planets by Holst on tape or CD

What you could do to follow up the story:

1. Act out the story using the props - create a moonscape outside, using a circular white blanket for the cardboard box 'rocket' to land on.
2. Ask the children to imagine they are going to fly into space and describe what they think it might be like.
3. Take the children into space, by imagining a space trip.
4. Help the children paint pictures of large scale planets with reflective paint, cut out silver stars and stick them on the walls of a large, dimly lit room. Use torches to explore your space.
5. Build a class space rocket using big cardboard boxes.
6. Pretend to fly into space, identifying the planets around you.
7. Land on the moon and go moon walking.
8. Make space rockets using junk. Paint or decorate them.
9. Help the children to organise a space picnic. Make space food and drinks. Tell space stories.

More stories to share

Stella to Earth by Simon Puttock and Philip Hopman - a story about a child's imaginary trip to the moon.

Moon Zoo by Carol Ann Duffy and Joel Stewart - a rhyming tale about a zoo on the moon.

Web sites

www.hamilton-trust.org.uk - select the Early Years tab for very detailed 'space' topic web, planning and printable resources.

www.sparklebox.co.uk - select 'numeracy' and 'space' for lots of themed resources including a free download of a rocket interactive whiteboard activity.

Links with the Early Learning Goals

PSD: Work as part of a group or a class.

CLL: Use language to imagine experiences.

KUW: Construct with a purpose in mind, using a variety of resources; find out about and identify features in the natural world.

PD: Experiment with different ways of moving.

CD: Begin to build a repertoire of songs; imitate and create movement in response to music.

How to Catch a Star

What's in the sky?

What you could put in the bag

* doll or figure to represent the little boy in the story
* plastic starfish or dried real one
* stars of different shapes, sizes & textured materials - fabric, foil, glittery, paper, laminated, plastic, luminous
* laminated pictures/posters about day and night and light and dark
* laminated examples of cubist style artwork
* geometric shapes or dough cutters - circles, squares, rectangles, stars
* laminated copy of Twinkle Twinkle Little Star

What you could do to follow up the story:

1. Act out the story using the props - create a beach using sand and water in a large tray outside. Explore the beach with bare feet.
2. Examine the different types of stars and describe their characteristics.
3. Go outside at different times in the day, make star shapes with bodies and create star shaped shadows.
4. Make star mobiles with foil, card, metallic paints, glitter..
5. Look at the shapes and describe their characteristics.
6. Examine the examples of artwork and encourage children to express views; use sponge circles, squares and rectangles to print lollypop trees.
7. Use day and night pictures as a starting point to talk about day and night.
8. Sing Twinkle Twinkle Little Star.
9. Look at photographs of real stars - find out what shape and colour they really are and what they are actually made of.

More stories to share

Laura's Star by Klaus Baumgart - beautifully illustrated and moving alternative star story.

The Star Who Fell Out of the Sky by Ian Robson & Ian Newsham - a star falls out of the sky and needs help to get back home.

Web sites

www.teachingideas.co.uk/earlyyears/files/twinkleurdu.doc - Twinkle Twinkle Little Star translated into Urdu.

www.nasa.gov - photographs and video footage of stars, planets, the universe and other galaxies, a wealth of information and pictures.

Links with the Early Learning Goals

PSRN: Use appropriate shapes to make pictures; select a particular named shape.

KUW: Describe simple features of objects; find out about the natural world.

PD: Move body position as necessary.

CD: Explore colour, shape, form and space in two dimensions; begin to build a repertoire of songs.

The Pig in the Pond

A problem ends in some fun

What you could put in the bag

* The Pig in the Pond on tape or CD
* a big cuddly toy pig and another made of plastic
* a farmer figure as Neligan
* a blue blanket or fabric to represent the pond
* a sun made from yellow card
* plastic farmyard animals - ducks, sheep, cows, chickens, dog, horse
* books about farm animals
* Old MacDonald farm game
* farmyard animal sounds listening lotto
* farming information video
* farm animal face masks

What you could do to follow up the story:

1. Act out the story. You could use plastic props or children dressed up using a paddling pool, or small world alternatives in a bowl of water. using the props - use plastic props and water tray or paddling pool outside and allow the children to create splashes.
2. Share the information book about farm animals to find out more about them.
3. Examine the toy farm animals. Look at features. Compare and contrast them. Categorise them.
4. Watch the video about farming, and find out about farm produce.
5. Examine and taste different farm produce. Match pictures of produce to relevant animals.
6. Visit a farm.
7. Talk about how the pig was feeling hot and ask the children to share their own experiences of swimming or water play on a hot day.

More stories to share

The Best Bottom by Brigitte Minne & Marjolein Pottie - a humorous story about a farmyard competition with a moral in the tale.

Cock-a-doodle-doo! Farmyard Hullabaloo by Giles Andreae & David Wojtowycz - book of short poems featuring a range of noisy farm animals.

Web sites

www.funwithspot.com - select 'farm games' for interactive matching pairs and dot-to-dot activities.

www.dltk-teach.com/books/farm/index.htm - a range of farm themed activities and story book suggestions.

Links with the Early Learning Goals

PSD: Be confident to try different farm produce; express likes and dislikes.

CLL: Use talk to reflect on past experience, linking significant events from own experience and from stories.

KUW: Find out and identify some features of living things and objects; look closely at similarities and differences.

The Rainbow Fish

About friendship

What you could put in the bag

* audio version of The Rainbow Fish
* soft or plastic toy Rainbow Fish
* other toy tropical fish
* some laminated scales - different colours, patterns, textures
* book about colours
* tub of tropical sorting fish
* colour matching game
* the Rainbow Fish matching pairs game
* information book about fish and the ocean
* fishing game
* Commotion on the Ocean poetry book

What you could do to follow up the story:

1. Act out the story using the props - do this outside using a deep perspex tank so that onlookers can see the fish moving under water.
2. Experiment with colour mixing.
3. Examine the laminated scales.Talk about colour, shape and texture.
4. Create multicoloured fish collages with scale shapes.
5. Paint pictures of the Rainbow Fish for a big collage.
6. Talk about sharing with each other and why this is so important. Discuss the moral of the story.
7. Examine the plastic tropical fish and discuss similarities, differences, colours and patterns.
8. Use computer art programs (e.g. Dazzle, Max's Toolbox) to create underwater fishy pictures using the 'fill' and 'stamp' tools.

More stories to share

The Leopard's Drum: An Asante Tale from West Africa by Jessica Souhami - a little leopard does not want to share his drum.

Sharing a Shell by Julia Donaldson & Lydia Monks - about sharing and friendship, featuring sea creatures.

The Selfish Crocodile and Other Animals by Faustin Charles, Michael Terry, Peter Blight, & Shen Roddie - four stories, each with a moral.

Web sites

www.naturegrid.org.uk/infant/earlyict - select 'stories' and 'Rainbow Fish' for a simple ICT lesson plan.

www.dltk-teach.com/books - scroll down to 'Rainbow Fish' for some craft ideas.

www.little-g.com/shockwave/games.html - select 'number aquarium' for an interactive counting game.

Links with the Early Learning Goals

PSD: Work as part of a group or class, taking turns and sharing fairly, understanding that there needs to be agreed values and codes of behaviour for groups of people to work together harmoniously.

KUW: Find out about and identify some features of living things.

CD: Choose particular colours to use for a purpose; explore what happens when they mix colours; make collages and paintings.

Dig Dig Digging

Explore diggers

What you could put in the bag

* toys to represent vehicles in the book - digger, fire engine, tractor, crane, dump truck, lorry
* a building site or city landscape mat
* books, DVDs etc. about different vehicles, work places and professions
* building materials to look at and use - cement powder, set cement, sand, stone, brick, gravel, bricks
* child-sized building tools - trowel, bucket, shovel, level
* building site or machinery puzzle
* hard hats and refelctive waistcoats

What you could do to follow up the story:

1. Act out the book using the props - do this outside in the sand area or a builder's tray.
2. Invite workers from various professions to come in with their machines.
3. Introduce stones, gravel and pebbles to the sand tray and set up a small world building site.
4. Look closely at the building material samples and talk about how and why they are used. Compare their weights.
5. Examine the tools and talk about their uses.
6. Set up a role play building site.
7. Use very large cardboard boxes to make vehicles and machines to be used in role play (a coating of PVA glue will strengthen them).
8. Use imagination to move bodies like different machines.
9. Design and make machines that have moving parts using junk.

More stories to share

The Amazing Machines series of books by Tony Mitton & Ant Parker are good alternatives for this story bag. They cover a wide range of vehicles including trucks, diggers and tractors and have rhyming text.

Web sites

http://ngfl.northumberland.gov.uk - select 'resources' and 'ICT' for interactive activities linked to the topic of building.

http://origin.bobthebuilder.com/uk - lots of interactive activities and games for children.

Links with the Early Learning Goals

CLL: Show an understanding of how information can be found in non-fiction texts to answer questions about why and how.

KUW: Ask questions about how things work; build and construct, selecting tools and techniques they need to shape, assemble and join materials; find out the uses of everyday technology.

PSRN: Use language such as 'heavier' and 'lighter' to compare quantities.

Greedy Zebra

Being part of a community

What you could put in the bag

* toy wild African animals for animals with colour and pattern - elephant, giraffe, snake, lion, crocodile, buffalo, lizard, monkey, leopard
* you could paint some with a single colours of paint to be the plain animals in the story
* a box for the cave
* toy white horse to represent the zebra without pattern and a patterned zebra
* animal patterned fabric cuttings to represent skins
* books of African animals
* wild animal lotto game or puzzle

What you could do to follow up the story:

1. Act out the story using the props - do this on a grassy area outside.
2. Create a Greedy Zebra display by making a path along a table leading to a cave on the wall. Use this to play out the story with small world animals.
3. Help the children to recreate the furs to hang in the cave by making animal patterns on pieces of cotton fabric using fabric crayons.
4. Make clay animals to represent the animals with no pattern or colour walking up to the cave.
5. Paint pictures of beautifully patterned animals and mount them as if they are leaving the cave.
6. Use information books to examine different wild animal colours and patterns; is there a reason why each animal is patterned/coloured in a certain way?
7. Discuss the moral of the story.
8. Encourage the children to create animal skin patterns of their own.

More stories to share

Crafty Chameleon by Mwenye Hadithi & Adrienne Kennaway - another story with a moral about a chameleon who uses his ability to change colour and hides from others.

Elmer by David McKee - also offers the opportunity for pattern work.

Web sites

www.sparklebox.co.uk - select 'topics', scroll down to 'natural world' and select 'animals and their habitats' for a set of illustrated safari topic words.

www.bbc.co.uk/nature/reallywild/amazing - good information source about a wide range of wild animals with clear photographs.

Links with the Early Learning Goals

PSD: Understand that different people have different cultures that need to be treated with respect.

KUW: Find out about and identify some features of living things.

PSRN: Talk about, recognise and recreate simple patterns.

CD: Explore colour, shape, form and space in two and three dimensions.

The Very Hungry Caterpillar

A story about growth (and greed!)

What you could put in the bag

* audio version DVD or video of the story
* soft green caterpillars of different sizes
* pictorial sequence or video featuring the life cycle of a butterfly
* information book about caterpillars and butterflies
* small plastic fruits and food items as featured in the story
* laminated butterfly matching game with butterflies cut in half
* tub of minibeasts for sorting

What you could do to follow up the story:

1. Act out the story using the props. You could do this outside in the garden or outdoor area.
2. Arrange the caterpillars in order of size.
3. Taste different fruits and talk about likes and dislikes.
4. Make a fruit cocktail and add some cocktail umbrellas and straws.
5. Examine different fruits and talk about similarities and differences.
6. Look closely at pictures of butterflies and talk about symmetry.
7. Use fruits cut in halves to print symmetrical patterns.
8. Use information books, pictures and video to find out about the life cycle of the butterfly.
9. Act out the stages of the lifecycle in music and movement.
10. Use a variety of materials to make model butterflies.
11. Copy Eric Carle's style and collage the Very Hungry Caterpillar using tissue paper.

More stories to share

The Crunching Munching Caterpillar by Sheridan Cain and Jack Tickle - a caterpillar eats to grow and longs to fly.

Web sites

www.naturegrid.org.uk/infant/earlyict - select 'seasons' and 'symmetrical butterflies' for a simple ICT lesson plan.

www.ltscotland.org.uk/earlyyears/index.asp - select 'resources' and 'illustrations' for a range of minibeast pictures.

www.train.stockton.gov.uk/pages/viewpage.asp?uniqid=4337 - go to 'English' for a sequencing activity for the interactive whiteboard.

www.dltk-teach.com/books - scroll down to 'Very Hungry Caterpillar' for a range of activity ideas.

Links with the Early Learning Goals

PSD: Be confident to try different fruits; express likes and dislikes.

PSRN: Count reliably up to 5 everyday objects; use language such as 'bigger' and 'smaller' to describe size; order items by size; talk about, recognise and recreate simple symmetrical patterns.

KUW: Find out about and identify some features of living things.

CD: Explore colour, texture, shape, form and space print patterns.

Flashing Fire Engines

More about mighty machines

What you could put in the bag

* a selection of toy fire engines
* small world fire fighting characters and equipment - hose, ladders etc
* books, pictures, videos, DVDs about fire fighting
* information book about fire safety
* different sized, shaped and scented candles
* fire engine puzzle
* emergency vehicle stencils or templates
* fire fighter outfit

What you could do to follow up the story:

1. Act out the book using the props - set up a fire rescue scenario outside with a doll's house, using real water.
2. Discuss fire safety.Talk about the fire drill at school and its purpose.
3. Set up a role play fire station.
4. Help the children write to the fire service and invite them to the setting or visit a fire station. Make a class book about the visit.
5. Talk about the history of fire. Why is it so important to life?
6. Look at a variety of candles burning; pretend to be flames - dance and move like fire.
7. Paint/draw pictures of fire engines.
8. Make model fire engines using junk.
9. Extend and find out about other emergency services (ambulance, sea and mountain rescue, police).

More stories to share

Fast Fire Engine by Jillian Harker - fun adventures of a fire engine.
Usborne Beginners: Fire Fighters by Katie Daynes - detailed and packed with facts.

Web sites

www.firemansam.co.uk/home.php - official website with interactive games, animated stories and a wide selection of activities for children.
www.welephant.co.uk - select 'fire safety' to open Welephant's website and access interactive games and an interesting animated story about the history of fire.

Links with the Early Learning Goals

PSD: Consider the consequences of their actions for themselves and others - in relation to fire safety.
CLL: Attempt writing for different purposes, using features of different forms - letter.
KUW: Ask questions about why things happen and how things work; find out about and identify the uses of everyday technology.

We're Going on a Bear Hunt

An old favourite

What you could put in the bag

* CD or DVD of We're Going on a Bear Hunt, Walker Books
* small world people to represent characters on the hunt
* soft toy brown bear
* information book about bears
* materials to represent different areas the characters pass through - artificial grass, a blue cellophane river, brown carpet mud, plastic trees,cotton wool snowstorm
* toy bears, a selection of different species

What you could do to follow up the story:

1. Act out the story using the props, puppets and soft toys or small world figures. Do this outside on a grassy patch, using a water tray, and a muddy area of soil and shrubbery.
2. Act out the story in a large space using a variety of apparatus and encourage the children to move appropriately as they are moving through the different obstacles described in the book.
3. Play word games using onomatopoeic words (words that sound like their meaning).
4. Examine the different species of toy bear and discuss similarities, differences and colours.
5. Find out about bears using information books.
6. Go on a nature trail that exposes the children to different types of terrain.

More stories to share

Walking Through the Jungle by Julie Lacome - opportunity for imaginative movement and plenty of onomatopoeic words.

Oscar's Half Birthday by Bob Graham - a family take their baby on a journey through their town and into the woods for a birthday picnic.

Web sites

www.naturegrid.org.uk/infant/earlyict - select 'journeys' and 'bear hunt' for an ICT lesson plan involving remote control or programmable toys.

www.literacymatters.co.uk - select 'early years' and 'term two' for Bear Hunt detailed plans. Also select 'resources' on the left to find downloadable pictures.

Links with the Early Learning Goals

KUW: Find out about and identify some features of living things; observe, find out about and identify features in the place they live and the natural world.

CLL: Explore and experiment with sounds, words and texts.

PSRN: Describe a simple journey.

PD: Move with confidence, imagination and safety; travel around, under, over and through balancing and climbing equipment.

CD: Play cooperatively as part of a group to act out a narrative.

The Night Pirates

A different sort of pirates

What you could put in the bag

* audio version of The Night Pirates, Egmont Books
* toy pirate ship
* figures to represent Tom, the three little girl pirates, Captain Patch and the four grown up pirates
* cardboard cut out of the front of a house, big enough to hide the ship
* treasure chest
* quarter moon with a face
* books about pirates
* black cardboard cut outs of pirates, monsters, trolls, ogres and pirate ships
* coins from different countries

What you could do to follow up the story:

1. Act out the story using the props - create darkness by throwing a blanket over some clothes driers outside.
2. Find a large empty space, black out the windows, shine lamps to create shadows and act out the story in a large space, encouraging the children to pretend they are pirates quietly moving in the darkness.
3. Set up a role play pirate ship or desert island.
4. Design and make pirate flags and fix them on lines, fences or climbing apparatus.
5. Use the cut out shapes of monsters, pirates and ships with a light box or overhead projector to experiment with silhouettes and shadows. Make up a shadow play
6. Look closely at the artwork in the book - create silhouette pictures.
7. Use rocks to make islands in the water tray and float toy pirate ships.
8. Examine the coins, talk about their features and the countries they come from.

More stories to share

Mr Jelly and the Pirates by Roger Hargreaves - Mr Jelly meets some pirates.

Jolly Roger by Colin McNaughton - Roger is kidnapped by pirates.

Web sites

http://ngfl.northumberland.gov.uk/Foundation - select the picture of the boat for an interactive ship jigsaw.

http://ngfl.northumberland.gov.uk/resources.html - select 'English' and 'The Little Red Ship' for an animated pirate story and word matching activity.

Links with the Early Learning Goals

CLL: Explore and experiment with sounds, words and texts.

KUW: Begin to know about other cultures (coins).

PSRN: Describe a simple journey; begin to recognise coins and use them in role play.

PD: Move with confidence, control, safety and imagination.

CD: Explore shape, form and space in two and three dimensions.

The Lighthouse Keeper's Catastrophe

More problems at the lighthouse

What you could put in the bag

* two dolls to represent Mr and Mrs Grinling
* model lighthouse, if possible, large enough for the dolls to enter
* books, pictures, DVD about light-houses and life as a lighthouse keeper
* information books about boats
* information books about lifeboats and sea rescue
* some small plastic boats
* objects for experimenting with floating and sinking
* torches

What you could do to follow up the story:

1. Act out the story using the props - set up the lighthouse on a large rock in a paddling pool outside.
2. Test different objects in a water tray to find out if they float or sink.
3. Challenge the children to build a boat that will float.
4. Use information books to compare different boat designs.
5. Test different materials to see if they are waterproof and will float.
6. Build boats and test in a paddling pool.
7. Share the information books about lighthouses.
8. Make a lighthouse using a real lamp.
9. Set up a role play lighthouse.
10. Make a PowerPoint presentation about lighthouses and encourage the children to imagine what it would have been like to be a lighthouse keeper.

More stories to share

Any of the books from the Lighthouse Keeper Series are good alternatives for this story bag.

Web sites

www.rnli-shorething.org.uk/Youth/default.aspx - education section of the RNLI website with lots of informative activities and games.

Links with the Early Learning Goals

PSRN: Use language such as 'heavier' or 'lighter' to compare weight.

KUW: Investigate objects and materials by using all of their senses as appropriate; ask questions about why things happen and how things work; build and construct with a side range of objects, selecting appropriate resources, and adapting their work where necessary; select the tools and techniques they need to shape, assemble and join the materials they are using; find out about and identify the uses of everyday technology to support their learning; find out about past events; observe.

PD: Handle tools, objects, construction and malleable materials safely and with increasing control.

CD: Work creatively on a small or large scale.

Book List

Jasper's Beanstalk - Nick Butterworth & Mick Inkpen
0-340-58634-6, Hodder Children's Books

Elmer - David McKee
0-09-969720-3, Red Fox

Dogger - Shirley Hughes
0-09-992790-X, Red Fox

The Black Geese - Alison Lurie, Jessica Souhami
0-7112-1444-1, Frances Lincoln

Handa's Surprise - Eileen Browne
0-7445-3634-0, Walker Books

Smiley Shark - Ruth Galloway
1-85430-862-9, Little Tiger Press

Cleversticks - Bernard Ashley & Derek Brazell
0-00-663855-4, Collins

The Gruffalo - Julia Donaldson & Axel Scheffler
0-333-71093-2, Macmillan

My Friend Bear - Jez Alborough
0-7445-6918-4, Walker Books

Jingle Bells - Nick Butterworth
0-00-664762-6, Collins

Not Now Bernard - David McKee
0-099-24050-5, Red Fox

My Friend Whale - Simon James
0-7445-9805-2, Walker Books

The Dance of the Dinosaurs - Colin & Jacqui Hawkins
0-00-711444-3, Collins

Owl Babies - Martin Waddell & Patrick Benson
0-7445-3167-5, Walker Books

Dear Zoo - Rod Campbell
0-333-71278-1, Campbell Books

The Big Wide-Mouthed Frog - Ana Martín Larrañaga
0-7445-9484-7, Walker Books

Titch - Pat Hutchins
0-14-050096-0, Puffin Books

Whatever Next! - Jill Murphy
0-333-63621-X, Macmillan

How to Catch a Star - Oliver Jeffers
0-00-715034-2, HarperCollins

The Pig in the Pond - Martin Waddell & Jill Barton
1-4063-0540-5, Walker Books

The Rainbow Fish - Marcus Pfister
1-55858-009-3, North-South Books

Dig Dig Digging - Margaret Mayo & Alex Aycliffe
1-84121-080-3, Orchard Picture Books

Greedy Zebra - Mwenye Hadithi & Adrienne Kennaway
0-340-40912-6, Hodder Children's Books

The Very Hungry Caterpillar - Eric Carle
0-140-56932-4, Puffin Books

Flashing Fire Engines - Tony Mitton & Ant Parker
0-7534-0298-X, Kingfisher

We're Going on a Bear Hunt - Helen Oxenbury & Michael Rosen
0-7445-2323-0, Walker Books

The Lighthouse Keeper's Catastrophe - David & Ronda Armitage
0-59011303-8, Scholastic

The Night Pirates
1-4052-1161-X, Egmont Books

Resources and further information

Early Learning Centre www.elc.co.uk 08705 352352

Tape measures; Buggy bins; tubs of minibeasts, sealife, farm; giant endangered species puzzle animals, dinosaurs, wild animals; under the sea puzzle; space quest mission squad; Pirate Island puzzle; fire accessory set; lacing animals in a tin; Funny Faces game; role play, small world; games/puzzles; wooden doll families; Old MacDonald's soundtracks game; wooden dolls house furniture; large animal snap cards; crates of plastic fruit/vegetables; Rain or Shine; play money; Bug buddies

Bright Minds www.brightminds.co.uk 08704 422144

Games/puzzles; sorting frogs; Splash attack; Ducks in a row; Pop to the shops; Listen and learn farm peg puzzle; UK money snap; Jack and the Beanstalk game; Dinosaur snap; Farmer's market; Colour and shape snap; Pig and piglet snap

Orchard Toys www.orchardtoys.com 01953 859520

Games; Puzzles: Cock-a-doodle-moo!; Farm- four in a box; Colour match express; Farm opposites; Crash, bang, wollop!; Farmyard; Farmyard dominoes; Giant farm; Jack and the Beanstalk; Jungle; Quack Quack; Mini jigs - shape and colour; Rain or shine; One, two, tree; Shape snap; Pets; Slug in a jug; Where in the wood?; Sneaky sharks; Who's in the jungle?; Wild world lotto; Who's on the farm?; Find the rhyme (puzzle game); Big fire engine; Big digger; Big pick and mix people tractor

Useful Websites...

National Literacy Trust www.literacytrust.org.uk
Storysack Ltd www.storysack.com
The Basic Skills Agency www.basic-skills.co.uk
Department for Education and Skills www.standards.dfes.gov.uk
The British Association for Childhood Education
www.early-education.org.uk

Sparkle Box www.sparklebox.co.uk
Amazon www.amazon.co.uk

Further reading

Foundations of Literacy: A Balanced Approach to Language, Listening and Literacy Skills in the Early Years, Sue Palmer and Ros Bayley, 2004, Network Educational Press (tel: 01202 665432 - website: www.networkcontinuum.co.uk)

The Little Book of Storytelling, Mary Medlicott, 2003, Featherstone Education (www.acblack.com/featherstone)

Literacy Outdoors: 50 Exciting Starting Points for Outdoor Learning Experiences, Ros Bayley and Lynn Broadbent, 2006, Lawrence Educational (tel: 0121 3443600 - website: www.educationalpublications.com)

A Few More Book Titles.

Little Teddy Left Behind by Anne Mangan & Joanne Moss
I Feel Sad by Brian Moses & Mike Gordon
Look Around You: The Toys We Play With by Sally Hewitt & Jane Rowe
DK Watch Me Grow: Elephant
Go Wild With Patterns, Neal Layton
Under the Sea by Fiona Patchett
Sharks by Catriona Clarke & Adam Relf
My Best Book of Sharks by Claire Llewellyn
The Deep Blue Sea by Jakki Wood
One Big Family by Ifeoma Onyefulu
One Child, One Seed by Kathryn Cave & Gisele Wulfsohn
Clever Gretchen and Other Forgotten Folktales by Alison Laurie
Favourite Russian Fairy Tales by Arthur Ransome
Pirates by Catriona Clarke
A New Home For a Pirate by Ronda Armitage & Holly Swain
My Shadow Poem by Robert Louis Stevenson
Let's Get a Pup! by Bob Graham
The Tiger Child: A Folk Tale from India by Joanna Troughton
In The Wild books written by Patricia Kendell
Flabby Tabby by Penny McKinlay & Britta Teckentrup
Dinosaur Roar by Paul & Henrietta Strickland
Harry and the Dinosaurs books by Ian Whybrow & Adrian Reynolds
Dinosaurs by Stephanie Turnbull
I Wonder Why Triceratops Had Horns DK Eye Wonder
Bears by Emma Fischel
Pete and Polo: Hide and Seek by Adrian Reynolds
Scary Creatures: Bears by Gerald Legg & Mark Bergin
Fiddle-i-fee by Jakki Wood
From Head to Toe by Eric Carle
This is the Sea That Feeds Us by Robert F Baldwin & Don Dyen
Rainbow Fish and the Big Blue Whale by Marcus Pfister
Whole World by Christopher Corr & Fred Penner
The Little Red Lighthouse & the Great Gray Bridge by Hildegarde H Swift
The Lighthouse Cat by Sue Stainton & Anne Mortimer

A letter to send to parents and carers...

School name and address

Dear Parent/Carer

We are currently collecting resources in order to make our own set of story bags.

Story bags contain favourite story books and a selection of props needed to bring them to life.

We and the children would be really grateful if you could have a look at home and see if you have any of the following objects:

____

____

Thank you very much for your help.

Kind regards,

____

The EYFS – Birth to Three

Little Baby Books offer lots of ideas for working with young children, and match the original birth to three framework.

A Strong Child | **A Skilful Communicator** | **A Competent Learner** | **A Healthy Child**

Set 1
978-1-905019-21-2

Set 2
978-1-905019-22-9

Set 3
978-1-905019-23-6

Set 4
978-1-905019-24-3

Also available with the activities grouped according to stage.

Book 1 Heads-up Lookers & Communicators (124pp)
978-1-905019-50-2

Book 2 Sitters, Standers & Explorers (156pp)
978-1-905019-51-9

Book 3 Movers, Shakers & Players (172pp)
978-1-905019-52-6

Book 4 Walkers, Talkers & Pretenders (238pp)
978-1-905019-53-3

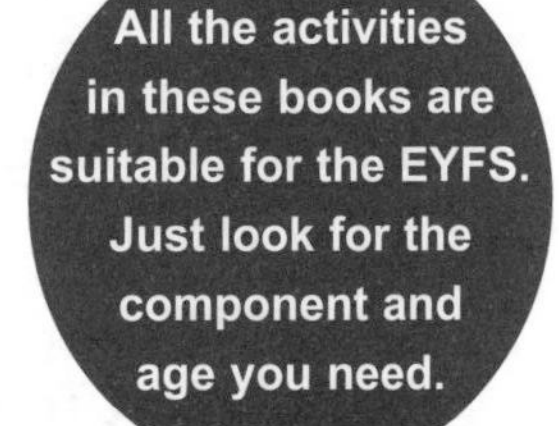

To see the full range of Featherstone books visit www.acblack.com

through the EYFS

Great for the Early Years Foundation Stage!

Ideal to support progression and extend learning.

Little Books with BIG Ideas®

The Little Book of Painting

Painting isn't just about brushes and powder paint. Painting can go on anywhere, inside or outside, and can involve spraying, splashing, printing, dripping, rolling – and hands!
This Little Book explores an imaginative range of painting activities using different sorts of materials and techniques, encouraging you and the children to experiment. It's beautifully illustrated with the author's own photographs taken in real settings.

ISBN 978-1-9060-2952-4

The Little Book of Story Bags

Story bags are widely used in the Foundation Stage. A story bag contains a focus story book, props and characters to act out the story, plus objects, resources and suggested activities. The idea is to use the story as a springboard to inspire creativity and imaginative role play.

You can buy story bags ready made, but it's also fun to make your own. This book will show you how.

ISBN 978-1-9060-2924-1

Visit our website for more details.

Order now for immediate delivery on publication.

Did you know that if you order on our website you get **everything you order with free postage and packing?**
Visit the website (www.acblack.com) or email littlebooks@acblack.com for information.